ADVANCED TACTICS IN
SPIRITUAL
WARFARE

BEYOND THE INSTITUTE OF SPIRITUAL
WARFARE, THE NEXT LEVEL

Prayer M. Madueke
BEST-SELLING AUTHOR OF MONITORING SPIRITS
& PRAYING WITH THE BLOOD OF JESUS

ISBN: 978-1-964584-06-5

Copyright © 2024 Prayer M, Madueke

All rights reserved. No part of this work may be reproduced or transmitted in any form or by any means without written permission from the publisher unless otherwise indicated.

All Scripture quotations are taken from the King James Version of the Bible, and used by permission. All emphasis within quotations is the author's additions.

Published by Prayer Publications.
Printed in the United States of America.

4 Free Ebooks

In order to say a 'Thank You' for purchasing *Advanced Tactics in Spiritual Warfare*, I offer these books to you in appreciation. Click or type madueke.com/free-gift in your browser.

Message from the Author

I want to see you succeed, grow, and break free from negativity and obstacles. My hope is for you to thrive, unaffected by negative influences and challenging situations. Because of that, please permit me to introduce two courses that I believe passionately will help you:

1. To break the evil altars and powers of your father's house, The role of altars in the realm of existence is very key because altars are meeting places between the physical and the spiritual, between the visible and the invisible.

    Unless a man cuts off the evil flow from the power of his father's house, he will not fulfil his destiny. Click here to learn more about my course on how to tear down unholy altars and close the enemy's entryways into your life!

2. To help you seamlessly break iron-like problems, illness, delayed marriage, poverty, or any long-standing battle.

    Discover the transformative power of Christian fasting and prayer. Remember, Matthew 17:21 teaches us, *"But this kind of demon does not go out except by prayer and fasting."* Ready to overcome your struggles? Click here to learn more about this course.

Embrace the journey ahead with faith, for through prayer, fasting, and the dismantling of evil altars, you shall unlock the doors to spiritual liberation and divine breakthrough. May your path be illuminated by His grace as you walk towards a life free from bondage.

If you're seeing this from the physical copy, type the link: madueke.com/courses in your browser to view all the courses on my website.

Christian Counselling

We were created for a greater purpose than only survival and God wants us to live a full life.

If you need prayer or counselling, or if you have any other inquiries, please visit the counselling page on my website to know when I will be available for a phone call.

Click or type links.madueke.com/counselling in your browser.

Let's Connect on Youtube

Join me on my YouTube channel, "Prayer M. Madueke," where I share powerful insights, guidance, and prayers for spiritual breakthroughs.

Subscribe today to unlock the secrets of the Kingdom and embrace an abundant life. Let's grow together!

Click or type links.madueke.com/youtube in your browser.

TABLE OF CONTENTS

Chapter One

Spiritual Warfare 1
How The Devil Defeats Some Believers 6
The Qualities Of Achan 7
The Weapons Of Our Warfare 9
What You Must Know..9
Divine Expectations From Believers...12
You Must Put On The Armor Of God 12
The Danger Of Walking In Dishonesty 13
What Do We Mean By Putting On The Armor? 15
Divine Ability, The Overcomers' Secret....................................17
Call For True Battle 18
God's Armor Consists Of:..20
The Beauty Of Our Warfare..20
What Is Fasting? 22
The Important Of Knowing God Before Fasting.....................23
God's Promise For Waiters Who Know Him 24
The God That Says We Should Wait 25
Search For God's Name 25
Insist In Knowing God Personally 26
Decision Before Action..29

Chapter Two

God's Names..32
The Lord God Of Abraham, Isaac And Jacob 32

God, The Only Strong One, Elohim 35
Power In The Name Of Jesus; The Elohim 35
How Demons Enter The Body 38
My Counsel 38
I Am That I Am 43
God's Redemptive Names For Your Deliverance 47
Our Father's Attributes 54

Chapter Three
Qualification Of God's Children And Wrong Prayers **57**
Praying With Love, Not With Hate 61
The Prayers Of A Repentant Wizard 64

Chapter Four
God's Attributes 1 .... **65**
The All Powerful Ominipotent, Infinite God 70

Chapter Five
God's Attributes 2 .... **72**
The Administrative Gift Of Moses' And David's Wisdom 72
Search For The Alpowerful God 76
The Ominipresent God 79

Chapter Six
God's Attributes 3 .... **81**
Encounter With Christ 83
The Immutability Of God 84
The Faithfulness Of Gofd 85
Determined Enemies And The Faithful God 87

ONE

SPIRITUAL WARFARE

- Everyone is in spiritual warfare, but it is only the genuinely born-again Christians who will be victorious.
- Being ignorant of the ongoing spiritual conflict in your life shows that you have already lost victory.
- The average man is defeated and overcome by sin and brought into bondage and slavery (Ephesians 6:12).
- This is why you cannot afford to be an average man.

I remember meeting a student one time who asked if we could just be everyday ordinary Christians instead of taking things seriously.

- The truth is that you cannot be ordinary or average. You must be on fire for God at all time.
- Many people, even some so-called believers, are overcome by one sinful character or another.

- Some powers bring them under such captivity, compelling them to do things they don't like.
- Some have accepted such a lifestyle and excuse themselves as being human.
- They are brought down into captivity and subjected to live under such sin till the day they die.
- When some believers allow themselves to be trapped by the lie of the devil that it is impossible to resist sin, such believers live like slaves to those sinful characters throughout their lives without putting up any resistance any longer (Galatians 5:17).
- God wants you to resist the devil and stand your ground against him at all times.
- Once you accept such sin in your life and fail to resist it, the devil will suppress and oppress you and eventually reign over all areas of your life.
- What the devil wants is for you to think it is impossible to resist sin, and that is also the desire of his principal demons, rulers of darkness and spiritual wickedness in the high places.
- The moment you accept sin in your life, these spiritual entities will try to take over your life and keep you trapped through manipulation and control.
- The will of God for you is to be redeemed, saved, and sanctified.
- Christ paid the total price for our redemption when he died on the cross (1 Peter 5:7-9; Luke 22:31).
- The implication of this is that you are not walking in the will of God if you still allow sin to have dominion over you (Rom 6:14).

- Victory over sin is the first victory that must be won in our spiritual warfare, without which every other victory and testimony is useless and empty.
- Once a man can attain victory over sin, every other victory quickly falls into place—victory over generational curses, victory over financial handicaps, victory over marital issues.
- Victory over sin restores the dominion man lost in the garden of Eden - Romans 5:12
- The moment you accept Jesus into your life as your Lord and savior, the first thing you must war against is sin.
- Sin is the major bottleneck and entanglement of every man. The temptations and enticement of sin have just one purpose – to destroy a man eternally.
- The book of Romans, specifically chapter 6:11, 12, exposes this concept.
- Believers are destined to overcome sin and Satan. This is achieved through the power of Christ's sacrifice and the power of the Holy Spirit (Matthew 13:19, 24-30).
- Until you reign over sin, you have yet to fulfil your destiny in Christ-likeness. According to the scripture, this is the truth we must know to be free.
- As a believer, you are not called to live a defeated life. That is not your destiny.
- You are called to live an empowered life that can withstand and resist the enemy's schemes.
- Evil spirits are attached to each sin we ever committed when we were sinners.

- At conversion, these spirits are cast out, but they try to reinforce to bring back those sins into our lives (Romans 7: 15).
- The beginning of spiritual warfare is to fight and keep yourself from being repossessed by those evil spirits in charge of those sins (2 Timothy 2:21; Luke 11:24-26).
- If a man becomes a honourable vessel, it becomes difficult for him to be used by unclean spirits.
- If you fail to fight these evil spirits, they will mess up your life with sinful characters, and this is what we call believers' warfare (1 Peter 5:8).
- When a man is sober, he is sensitive. Sensitivity helps one to recognize the baits of sin and Satan. A sober man is also sensitive to the voice of the Holy Spirit.
- At salvation, life's actual battles begin, and this fight is called a good fight of faith.
- It is first a fight of faith because all that the devil truly is after in the life of a man is his faith. The Bible says the just shall live by faith. This means when there is no faith, a man is not just.
- Salvation is the beginning of every believer's warfare against our adversary, the devil who still walks about seeking believers to devour with sin and its consequences.
- It was not until Jesus was baptized by John the Baptist and heard the confirmatory voice from heaven that the devil came to tempt.
- Once you become confirmed by heaven through salvation, get ready to face the temptations of the devil.

- If you say you are born again, your profession (of being born again) will be tested; that's the trial of the faith you confess (1 Peter 5:7-9; Luke 22:31).
- The devil doesn't believe you until he tests your confession of faith;
- The believer's salvation is confirmed by both heaven and hell after the believer's warfare against sin.

- If you allow evil spirits in charge of sin to repossess you after being born again, the battle or spiritual warfare will be doubled.
- It's called 'WARFARE WITHOUT' and 'DEPRAVITY WITHIN' and this makes our warfare very difficult.
- But when there's no sin within, you can fight with ease and victory is sure (Numbers 23:21, 23).
- Unfortunately, many believers believe that the battle is fought and finished at salvation without passing through tests or trials of their confession - such ignorance is very dangerous (1 peter 5:7-9; Luke 11:24-26).
- Such ignorant believers are easily overcome by sin through demonic resistance against their faith. You should read that again.
- The powers behind every sin you overcame at salvation can try to come back through human weakness and frailty, your neighbors' bad examples, and sinful people among weak believers.
- If you pitch your tents near Sodom, that is, hang out with old sinful friends, and spend so much time with people in the far country, you will never be victorious (2 Corinthians 6:14-18).

- If you are too accessible to sin- fleshly desires, and worldly ambition, you will not fight well unto victory.

- If after salvation you forget that there's a warfare going on, you will be defeated.
- Every believer is a soldier on a battlefield expected to put on the whole armor of God.

HOW THE DEVIL DEFEATS SOME BELIEVERS

- To defeat some believers, the devil will try to cause indolence among them to hinder their ability. his weapons of attack include making a believer doubt God's word, misinterpret it, or ignore it.
- He may also cause the believer to forget the word of God he heard (Matthew 13:3-9).
- He may attack you with spiritual slumber or plant some things inside you while you sleep physically and spiritually.
- The devil does this to make sure the believer does not have enough of God's word to fight (Matthew 13:19, 24-26).
- God's word is needed to fight the devil as seen in Matthew 4 during the temptation of Jesus Christ in the wilderness.
- In times of warfare, he uses people, things, and circumstances available to resist the faith of believers by all means (Joshua 7:21; Genesis 3:1-6).

- He may fight you through the corruption of the human heart, through the mind and eye gate, or through the influence of an evil companion, a close acquaintance, and people of class and wisdom (1 Corinthians 15:33; Proverbs 22:24-25).
- The eye gate of Achan was opened by the enemy in the war front and without minding the reign of bullets, he coveted what he was supposed to destroy (Exodus 14:26-31; Exodus 12:29, 30; 9:25-26).

THE QUALITIES OF ACHAN

- Achan was a man that survived many wars and possibly, the task masters of Egypt under the supervision of Pharaoh.
- This was a man who was probably born in Egypt during the time of the Egyptian bondage; attacked, but survived the magicians and sorcerers who used enchantment against the children of Israel in Egypt.
- Achan must have been around when the red sea was in the way of the Israelites and saw the miraculous divine intervention.
- He must have seen many miracles and eaten manna in the wilderness.
- He must have seen the Egyptian soldiers destroyed in the red sea.
- He must have seen how the power of God healed the bitter water, rained manna in the wilderness, overcame the great Amalek (Exodus 15:22-23, 25, 26; 16:1-4, 12-18, 21-25, 31-35; 17:1-16).
- Even if Achan was not among the ten spies sent to spy Jericho, he knew them by their names.

- He was around when the wall of Jericho collapsed.
- He knew what happened to all the first-born males during their last night in Egypt.
- He was aware of the plagues in Egypt - how hail smote many of them except Goshen, the land where the Israelites occupied.
- He was there when God judged and killed Nadab and Abihu and why He did so.
- He was a trained soldier who fought gallantly at Rephidim until they prevailed and discomfited the Amalek (Exodus 17:8-16).
- Achan was enlisted as one of the great soldiers that fought King Arad and utterly destroyed their cities.
- He fought the Amorites, smote them with the edge of the sword and possessed their land from Aron unto Jabbok.
- However, all these did not stop him from committing atrocity.
- It is important to guard your eyes as a believer.
- He was among the soldiers that fought and smote Bashan until there was none left alive and they possessed their land (Numbers 21:1-3, 21-32, 33-35; 25:16-18; 31:1-24; Acts 1:16-20).
- He took them but never used them because he was stoned by his fellow soldiers.
- Be not deceived, evil communications corrupt good manners. Avoid those who encourage you to look at forbidden things lustfully.

THE WEAPONS OF OUR WARFARE

- You must know that there is a great warfare which everyone must face, especially believers.
- The scripture clearly states that the world is a battle ground between God's children and Satan's agents.
- Once you repent and raise the banner of the King of kings anywhere, the devil will become furious with you.
- The main aim of the devil's fight against you as a believer is to bring you under subjection, in order to obey the laws in the territory they claim to own.
- Another aim of his is to make sure the believer is not in right standing with God, the Father.
- He desires to always find something to use against the believer before the Father (John 14:30).
- It's important to grasp that the Christian journey is often likened to warfare, wrestling, and fighting (2 Corinthians 10:3-5; 1 Corinthians 15:30-32; Ephesians 6:12).

WHAT YOU MUST KNOW

- If there's no battle to fight and war to engage in, Paul would have told us otherwise (Ephesians 4:18; Jeremiah 17:9; Romans 7:18).

- "There's a stronghold to pull down right within our heart to bring light in our darkened understanding.
- There's a stronghold built by the devil in our human mind.
- We need to destroy the powers of darkness in our minds and defiled conscience. We need to liberate our deceived heart that's desperately wicked.
- Our warfare begins within ourselves, in the battleground of our hearts and minds to conquer the effect of the fallen man nature within us.
- Believers are called to fight and pull down the old man, the body of sin, the carnal nature, the flesh and every filthiness right inside us as stated in Ephesians 4:22-24.
- We must destroy and completely pull down the inward enemy, the dominating tyrant and the mortal nature from the root (1 Timothy 6:12; 1 Corinthians 9:25-27).
- Every rooted evil imagination, every high thing and evil forces that reign over us must be cast out. All bad character in us must be brought down to obey Christ.
- We mustn't give up like Achan but we must fight a good fight of faith.
- We must strive for mastery to obtain an incorruptible crown.
- We mustn't beat the air or run this race with uncertainty.
- We must bring our body under divine control and submission to God's will to avoid the mistake Achan made. Apostle Paul made this clear in 1 Corinthians 9:26-27.

- In Ephesians 6:12, the Bible makes us understand that there are spiritual invisible forces fighting to bring believers down to disobey God.
- The people we see in our midst doing wrong things physically are the agents of those invisible forces.
- Among these are deceitful spirits and false teachers who propagate lies and lead people astray. They are not our main enemies, source or the strongholds of our conflict.
- These evil forces plant into the evil imaginations of their agents to fight God's knowledge in God's children.
- They also possess their agents through various means, including deception, manipulation, and yielding to sinful desires.
- They want the knowledge of God to die so that they can establish their evil knowledge here on earth.
- That's why they use their human agents to fight believers who have the knowledge of God.

DIVINE EXPECTATIONS FROM BELIEVERS

- Believers should arm themselves with the resources provided by God to fight, wrestle, war and defeat them here on earth.
- Believers can guard against demonic influence by staying rooted in God's Word, cultivating a vibrant prayer life, and surrounding themselves with fellow believers for support and accountability (James 4:7).

YOU MUST PUT ON THE ARMOR OF GOD

- The armor of God is of paramount importance for believers in spiritual warfare (Ephesians 6:10, 11, 13).
- The armor includes the belt of truth, breastplate of righteousness, shoes of the gospel of peace, shield of faith, helmet of salvation, and sword of the Spirit.
- Without the armor of God, believers are vulnerable to the enemy's attacks and strategies.
- Believers have all the armor provided by God to fight every spiritual warfare.
- When you put on this armor and use them rightly, then you will be sure of victory.
- Without putting on the whole armor, you will not be strong to fight and will surely lose the war.

- Before you can start fighting and become strong in the Lord, you must have died to sin and become alive unto God.
- Victory over sin brings believers nearer to harvest the benefits of salvation and without this, you may profess salvation but will not harvest its benefits (Romans 6:11, 12).

THE DANGER OF WALKING IN DISHONESTY

- Without victory over sin, you may learn how to pray, how to prosper, sow seed and keep every other Christian doctrine without harvesting the benefits of your salvation.
- It is good to repent and forsake your sins, but if you fail to keep your salvation, you will not harvest its benefits.
- Just as seed planting is important in farming, harvesting what you planted is also very important 1 John 1:9).
- Believers who commit sin after salvation are called to awake from sleep and cast off the works of darkness (Romans 13:11-14).
- Believers who walk in dishonesty are called to amend their ways.
- Believers who now engage in rioting, drunkenness, chambering, in wantonness, strife and envy must stop, if they must harvest the seed of salvation they planted.
- They are called to put on Christ and make no more provision for the flesh, to fulfill their lusts as stated in Romans 13:14.
- Believers are called never to go back to lying but to put off every evil deed (Colossians 3:9-14). They are called to put on the new lifestyle, not the old sinful lifestyle.

- Believers are called to represent Christ in this sinful world.
- God's elect should possess God's nature like humility, show of mercy, kindness, meekness, etc.
- God have given us his nature and has provided us with weapons to fight, so there's no need to search for it.
- The resources and power are available already. No believer has any excuse to live an impotent, cold, fruitless life.
- The problem with many believers is ignorance and inability to appropriate the weapons and remain obedient to God.
- To win, you must obey God's word and fight along with Him because you cannot win without Him.
- Spiritual warfare cannot be fought and won by human techniques; you can only win the war by fighting with the whole of God's armor on (Zechariah 4:6; James 4:6-7).
- With the fruits of the Holy Ghost and submission to God in place, if you resist the devil, he must flee.

WHAT DO WE MEAN BY PUTTING ON THE ARMOR?

- Without putting on the whole armor in obedience, people who seemed to be strong and courageous in the past have fallen victims in the day of spiritual warfare.
- No matter how strong, intelligent and powerful you look, if you fail to put on the armor in obedience, you will fail woefully in the day of battle.
- Our only hope of victory is to put on the whole armor because self-confidence will disappoint you.
- The only effective and sufficient weapon is God's grace and armor, not your strength or help from anyone (2 Corinthians 12:9; Ephesians 6:13-18).
- A believer should be vigilant because the territory where we live is dominated by unbelievers.
- We must be vigilant and not pretend as if there's no battle to fight.
- If you are lazy and neglect to prepare and fight, you will be taken captive.
- Once you hear God's word, don't postpone it; act immediately (Luke 8:12; 2 Corinthians 4:3-4). That's what we mean by putting on the armor and being obedient.
- Any delay can empower the devil to weaken your faith, blind your eyes or steal the word of God completely.
- Taking away the word of God from you or causing you not to obey is one of Satan's dangerous strategies.
- You must study the scriptures to avoid being a novice but to become well equipped with God's word for effective battle.

- Without the above, the devil will cause you to magnify yourself and bring you into his trap; cause you to take wrong decisions, to make painful mistakes, and get you into scandals, reproach, disgrace and shame (1 Thessalonians 2:18; 1 Timothy 3:6, 7)/

DIVINE ABILITY, THE OVERCOMERS' SECRET

- The divine armor on you and the consciousness that a battle is going on is the assurance that you will win in every battle.
- If the devil or his agent succeeds in convincing you to believe that there's no battle going on or that there's nothing like spiritual warfare, you are defeated already.
- Every believer is in heaviness brought by the devil and his agent through manifold temptations.
- He is fighting every believer to prevent us from having access to our incorruptible inheritance that cannot fade away (1 Peter 1:3-9).
- Our faith as believers must be tried by the devil here on earth before we can have access to our undefiled possession.
- The beginning of our faith in Christ doesn't give us final victory without trials and temptations through warfare until the end.
- Believers can fall many times and rise at the beginning of their faith but at the end of the last victory, they shall never fall.
- If any believer falls at the last, all his past victories will not bring his soul into the everlasting kingdom of our Lord Jesus Christ (2 Peter 1:10-11).
- As a believer, you cannot be deeply involved with the affairs of this life without having eternity in view and still become a good soldier of Christ.
- An army cannot fight two different wars and win successfully at the same time. Immediately you die or the rapture takes place, all that you are fighting for now without Christ will become worthless in the reality of eternity.

- We are called to do everything whatever we are doing having eternity in view, here and now.
- You must guard your heart against the love of money, fame, evil pleasure and covetousness in everything you do in life (2 Timothy 2:3-4; 1 Timothy 6:10-12).
- Having victory over the works of the flesh is fighting the good fight of faith (Hebrews 12:1-4; Matthew 5:28-30; Hebrews 10:25; 1 John 5:4-5; Revelation 2:11).

CALL FOR TRUE BATTLE

- Born again Christians are called to lay aside and put off anything that will bring us back into a life of sin; this is the second deliverance.
- There are more kingdoms to conquer after salvation. It's after this that believers will begin to enjoy their salvation.
- We must continuously look unto Jesus and believe in Him to finish the work He started with us at salvation.
- Believers who claim God's grace to fight other powers but neglect the grace that fights the return of sin after salvation are not fighting the good fight of faith.
- If you are carrying the real cross, there's something to fight, things to endure, shame to despise and contradictions to overcome.
- Those who got married and overcame fornication still have to overcome adultery and other sexual perversions.

- Those who have conquered outward sin still have internal sins to overcome.
- The secret sin many must avoid is evil communication or association to enable us to have proper identification with believers (1 Peter 2:11).
- You cannot be in the midst of people with contradicting faith and fight the good fight of faith.
- Believers are called to guide their faith jealously, which is more precious than the whole world.
- Our faith is a priceless treasure which we must hold fast.
- We must fight never to exchange our faith with anything.
- Believers who underestimated the devil's craftiness fell in the day of battle because they didn't appropriate God's armor.

GOD'S ARMOR CONSISTS OF:

- The breast plate of truth (Ephesians 6:14; Luke 12:35; 1 Peter 1:13).
- The breastplate of righteousness (Ephesians 6:14; 1 Peter 1:14-16).
- The shoes of the gospel of peace (Ephesians 6:15; Romans 1:16-17).
- The shield of faith (Ephesians 6:16; Hebrews 11:32-34; 1 Peter 5:9; 1 John 5:4).
- The helmet of salvation (Ephesians 6:17; 1 Thessalonians 5:8).
- The sword of the Spirit (Ephesians 6:17; Matthew 4:1-11; Psalms 119:11; Hebrews 4:12; 1 Peter 3:15).

THE BEAUTY OF OUR WARFARE

- The beauty of our warfare is that once you abide in God, He promises never to leave us alone to fight against the enemies in the battle field.
- Our defender, the Lord Jesus has passed through the fires of betrayals, deception, conspiracy, injustice, evil devise and whatever we are going through or will ever go through.
- The comforting word is that He will help us. If you remain royal, obedient and faithful to the end, He will satisfy you and bless you immensely.
- As we resist the devil, separate ourselves from the tempters by closing every gate through which temptations comes and keep

praying for divine grace, we shall have victory (1 Corinthians 10:13; Hebrews 2:18; Psalms 34:19; Isaiah 43:1-2).

WHAT IS FASTING?

- The dictionary meaning of fasting simple means; *to abstain from food, to eat sparingly or abstain from some food.*
- In the scripture, Jesus fasted for forty days and forty nights without food and water (Matthew 4:2; Luke 4:2; Matthew 15:32; Mark 8:1-3; Jonah 3:5-7).
- From the above text, Jesus decided not to eat and drink in other to fast and pray.
- During the fasting, Jesus ate nothing throughout the period He fasted (Mark 6:7, 20; Esther 4:16; Acts 27:33).

The multitude who followed Him for about three days didn't eat because they had no food to eat. That's not real fasting. If you don't have time to eat because of your busy schedule, it's not biblical fasting.

- Biblical fasting is praying without eating any food or drink.
- It could mean skipping one meal to have enough time to pray.

THE IMPORTANT OF KNOWING GOD BEFORE FASTING

- Fasting is creating time to seek the face of God in order to pray effectively (Isaiah 40:25-31).
- It's waiting upon God and before you do this, you have to know the God you want to seek.
- Prophet Isaiah challenged the children of Israel to know God before waiting on Him.
- Whom you equal God to in your heart is a very important question that needs an answer before waiting for Him.
- You need to look around you to admire God's handiwork and everything that God created.
- All things known and unknown to you are God's creation and He knows them and called them by their names.
- He is mighty and strong in power and can never fail.
- He knows you and your ways in detail. He is everlasting; the only creator that no one created whose understanding is unlimited.
- You must know that the God you want to wait on is all powerful and can never be weary, but increases in strength.
- He gives power to the faint and those that has no might, He increases their strength (Isaiah 40:29).
- All creation is bound to faint, grow weary, get old and expire, but God never faints or grows weary.

GOD'S PROMISE FOR WAITERS WHO KNOW HIM

- But He has promised that they that wait upon the LORD shall renew their strength (Isaiah 40:31; Exodus 8:10; 15:11; 39:6).
- After renewal, they shall mount up with wings, not like other birds, but as eagles.
- They shall run and not be weary; and they shall walk, and not faint.
- Before you can seek God through fasting and find Him, you have to know Him and his thoughts about you.
- You have to know his concern; how great and powerful He is.
- Our God has no comparison, none to be equal to Him in any ramification.
- You must understand without divided mind that He is greater than the greatest and more powerful than the most powerful among the creatures.
- It's foolishness to liken God to anything, animate or inanimate put together.
- He is bigger than the biggest. All gods bow before Him and his holiness is glorious, fearful in praises and wonders.
- He created everything in heaven and on earth; He created the sons of the mighty and none can match Him, compare unto Him or be likened unto Him.
- Who's the God that says we should wait for Him?

THE GOD THAT SAYS WE SHOULD WAIT

- If the gathering of the presidents of the world asks you to wait on them, you will consider it more important to any other thing.
- If an enemy, someone you don't know or one who is unprofitable to you ask you to wait for him, you may not consider it very important (Exodus 3:13, 10-12, 2, 13).

If you are told that someone asked you to wait for him, you will like to know the person first. Knowing the name of the person will determine whether you are going to stay or not.

SEARCH FOR GOD'S NAME

So, let us search for God's name to understand who is asking us to wait for Him through fasting and prayer (Genesis 32:9, 29).

- Remember, Moses ran away from Egypt to save his life from Pharaoh.
- Now, someone he doesn't know His name is telling him to go back to Egypt.
- In addition, the person told him to meet with Pharaoh, not just to go back to Egypt.
- Another very important thing is that this person was going to become Israel's source of deliverance from the Egyptian bondage.

- Moses had been in the palace for forty years and understood both Pharaoh and the Egyptians.
- They were very powerful, wicked, merciless, unforgiving and can kill with no feeling of guilt.
- Pharaoh and the highest court of the Egyptians condemned Moses to death and so, they were looking for him to kill.
- Now someone he didn't know very well neither did he know His name is saying he should return with an assignment to deliver a whole nation who was in bondage and the source of the national economy.
- The only thing that made Moses give attention to this discussion was the encounter he had with the burning bush- the bush was on fire, but it was not consumed!

INSIST IN KNOWING GOD PERSONALLY

- Before Moses could accept such an assignment which was worse than a suicide mission, he insisted on knowing the name of the person sending him.
- When God told Jacob to return back to his father's house while Esau was alive, he demanded for His name.
- With these examples, it's therefore good for you to know the name of the God who is asking you to wait on Him through fasting and prayer.

- The reason why many people who wait on God complain, grudge, become impatient and wait in vain is because they don't know God (Acts 7:21-22, 29-32).
- It's good to take time to study about God- who He is, what are His names, attributes and what He can do before waiting on Him through prayer and fasting.
- Moses didn't move out to carry out divine assignment until he discovered God's name.
- He needed to know the name just in case the children of Israel ask him.
- This will help him and the children of Israel to know the power and the authority of the one sending him.
- Likewise, you need to know the power and the authority behind the person that is asking you to wait on Him in prayer and fasting.
- People enter into ministry, business and other ventures rashly without being sent or knowing who sent them.
- That's why when problem arise, they run up and down until the devil traps them with counterfeit help.
- It's of no use waiting on someone who will not defend you in times of trouble.
- Moses knew the history of the Egyptians and the children of Israel in details.
- He cannot just return to Egypt without assurance that the power and authority sending him back is bigger than that of the Egyptians.
- Most times, people make the decision to do things just by trial without assurance.

- It's wrong to go into fasting without the assurance that your prayers will be answered.

DECISION BEFORE ACTION

- Abel was sure that his sacrifice would be accepted by God before he engaged himself in carrying out such sacrifice.
- That was why he refused to compromise with his brother Cain even unto death (Genesis 4:2-4, 8).
- Abel knew that his sacrifice will please God and bring respect to him.
- Even when his brother threatened to kill him, he didn't budge.
- If you are going to join us in this fasting, in waiting upon God, you must be convinced with unshakeable decision (Genesis 5:13-14, 22).
- When Noah took decision to build the ark, he was convinced that he was doing the right thing.
- As a result, he invested all that he had and did all that God told him to do.
- Noah was the only person who didn't cry, regret or die in the time of trouble.
- His generation perished for not obeying God's word because they never believed that God was able to save the world through the ark.
- Also, those who joined Noah were saved because they believed God (Genesis 12:1-9).
- If you must join us to wait on God in this program, you must know God.
- Abraham answered the call of God because he believed that God is able to keep the promises, He made to him.
- It took time, but God's promises never fail, it must come to pass (Joshua 21:43-45).

- Abraham never struggled over anything because he believed that no power can take from him what God promised him (Genesis 13:1-4, 8-18).
- Because of that knowledge, he always waited on God. To maintain peace, he allowed Lot to choose where he wanted to live and God strengthened his promise to him thereafter.
- The enemy fought God's promises to Abraham but because he knew God, he never stopped waiting on Him.
- While waiting, he entertained angels, rescued Lot from his captors; kept the doctrine of circumcision and prayed for Sodom and Gomorrah (Genesis 21:1-5).
- At the end, the God he waited for never disappointed him, even at his old age.
- If God says to you wait, you better wait because at His arrival every knee must bow.
- When God assured Jacob to leave Laban, he defended him before his worst enemy, Esau (Genesis 33:1, 4, 20).
- His elder brother who vowed to destroy him with about four hundred soldiers withdrew from his decision.
- This could only be possible when Jacob waited on the God that can do all things.
- Instead of a fight, his brother Esau changed his mind; he embraced him, fell on his neck, kissed him and they both wept for joy.
- This can only happen by obeying God's invitation to wait in prayer and fasting.
- Prayer and fasting can reverse evil intentions and cause your enemies to favor you.

- Those who know their God can wait, no matter how long (Isaiah 8:17; Job 17:9).

TWO

GOD'S NAMES

THE LORD GOD OF ABRAHAM, ISAAC AND JACOB

- When Moses enquired of God's name, He told him, I am the LORD God of your fathers, the God of Abraham, the God of Isaac, and the God of Jacob.
- Moses knew the history of Israel very well and all Israel believed that it's only the God of Abraham, Isaac and Jacob that can deliver them from Pharaoh and the Egyptian bondage.
- They had prayed and expected such deliverance and had been waiting for His intervention (Exodus 3:15' 6:3).
- He is the God that entered into covenant with Abraham and fulfilled it in the midst of impossibilities (Genesis 3:6-8).
- They had done so many things to escape the bondage of Pharaoh but failed.
- Their only hope of freedom is God and they had cried endlessly to Him in their prayers.

- Immediately Moses heard of this name his faith was quickened and he believed God.
- More so, this is the only name the children of Israel were waiting for to escape the Egyptian bondage.
- In the time of hopeless situation, this same God appeared to Abraham, Isaac and Jacob by the name JEHOVAH.
- In every situation, whenever this name appeared, no power stands or questions his authority (Ephesians 2:19-20).
- So, to Moses and the children of Israel, their deliverance is assured with this name in the battle field.
- The primary reason why many remain in their bondage today is that they don't know how God appears to them. But I can help you know if only you can believe.
- Listen to me, most great men of God you hear of in the scripture or wish to meet today physically are not better than some of us in any way.
- The reason why people in their generation were delivered is because they believed in what they told them.
- You have only one step to your deliverance and that step is for you to believe what I am telling you here and now.
- If you will stop whatever you are doing now, repent of all your sins, ask God to forgive you all your known and unknown sins, your deliverance will be unlocked.
- If you will determine to forsake those sins, ask Christ to come into your live and take over, you are on the path of total freedom.
- In this program, as you read and pray the prayers attached to this book, your bondage will be broken.

- Through this program, your own God of Abraham, Isaac and Jacob has appeared; only believe.
- Immediately Moses confirmed the reality of the name that appeared to him, he boldly left for Egypt to confront Pharaoh (Galatians 1:1; Psalms 91:1).
- Now that you are hearing this name, you can confront and conquer your Pharaoh.
- The God we are talking about is the father of our LORD Jesus, who can raise the dead and quicken mortal bodies.
- His name is the Almighty with no minus to his mightiness.
- As you go to Him in prayer after you have genuinely repented, He will break your bondage.
- There's safety in abiding in his presence and in dwelling in his secret place.

GOD, THE ONLY STRONG ONE, ELOHIM

- Do you know that the word ELOHIM, which is translated God is used about 2,500 times in the Old Testament and it means "THE STRONG ONE".
- No true Israelite jokes with the name of Abraham, Isaac and Jacob, likewise true Christians.
- Once that name is mentioned, victory is assured and bondages are broken.
- The name Almighty God is a threat to the devil and all his agents put together.

POWER IN THE NAME OF JESUS; THE ELOHIM

- Let me reveal to you one important secret: Do you know that all the names of God the father is inside Jesus?
- If you don't know before, begin to use the name of Jesus to break your bondage now that you know.
- When Christ came to this world fully equipped with these names, He broke every bondage (Matthew 4:23-25).
- Through this name, He healed all manner of sicknesses and diseases.
- As He was teaching people about the Almightiness of God, preaching the gospel of the kingdom, all those who were possessed were delivered (Matthew 8:1-4).

- Devils were cast out, lunatic destroyed and people with palsy were set free at the mention of the name of Jesus.
- For the first time since the time of Moses, a leper was cleansed when he listened to the sermon of Christ.
- Immediately Christ saw that this leper believed Him, He said, be clean and that was all.
- As you read this book and pray the prayers in it, Christ is watching you (Matthew 8:16-17).
- Immediately your faith is confirmed, no bondage will hold you down.
- What you are hearing is the word of Christ, not mine, so start believing and your problem will be solved.
- If you are the type that seeks prophecies, what you are hearing now is prophetic.
- I prophesy that as many as are reading this book, I command the demons behind your problem to be cast out, in the name of Jesus (Matthew 8:1-3).
- The word you are hearing now can cast out any unclean spirit troubling you and heal every part of your body under satanic attack.
- There are people whose attack comes from the grave yard and at times they see themselves with the dead (Matthew 8:23-24, 26).
- They eat and drink foods cooked in satanic kingdom in their dreams.
- Some are suffering the same sickness, poverty, hardship their parents suffered. Jesus with the name Almighty dealt with such evil forces.

- There are other people who suffer disaster, great storms and losses. The ship of their lives carrying their wealth is under demonic arrest.
- With the name God Almighty, Elohim or the strong one, you can overcome.
- For some others, as soon as they are about to make it to the next level, great storms, fire outbreak strikes and waste their life time efforts.
- Today, Jesus will arise and rebuke your storms and your life, business and everything you do here on earth will experience great calm (Luke 6:6, 10).
- There are people whose hands are demonized and anything they touch never prospers.
- If they give such hand in marriage, it will not work but today, all these things will become things of the past if only you believe.
- With the name Elohim, translated God, the strong one, you will be delivered.
- Demons enter into human body to cause all manner of problem.

HOW DEMONS ENTER THE BODY

- When demons enter the body, they cause people to be sick, weak and confused. At times they bring fear, lack, poverty, sufferings and deaths (James 4:7).
- Most times they enter through sin or by evil consultation with their agents or people who have familiar spirits.
- If you are attached to false prophets, witch doctors or any satanic agent, demons can possess you.
- Most of these prophets are demonized and they practice fortune telling and hypnotism.
- Whichever way they enter, their aim is to oppress their victim if they fail to resist them.
- The only way to resist them is through hearing what you are hearing now and by prayer.
- Submit yourselves therefore to God. Resist the devil, and he will flee from you (James 4:7).

MY COUNSEL

- By the time you finish this program, I have a counsel to give you.
- I am convinced that your bondage will be broken after this program but one thing is very important- avoid sin.
- The problem with many deliverance ministers and deliverance candidates is rooted in their inability to leave sin alone.

- This must be emphasized if you must keep your deliverance and enjoy abundant life.
- As you repent, confess your sins and forsake them, God's Spirit with all his names enters into you.
- If you go back to sin, God's Spirit leaves you and evil spirit enters and takes over you (John 5:14).
- This is one of the most important pieces of information you need as you pray the prayers in this book.
- God's Spirit doesn't stay in the same body or place with demons (1 Samuel 16:14-15).
- If you want God's presence, stay away from sin and keep yourself clean.
- You may be asking; how do I achieve this? Let's see how Peter and Paul counselled the believers in their time.

HOW TO BE REALLY DELIVERED

- Peter wrote to his deliverance candidates in 1 Peter 5:8, to be sober and vigilant just as I am writing to you now.
- You ask why? The reason is because the demon you cast out is not dead, no matter how much you pray for them to die (1 Peter 5:8-9; Ephesians 4:27).
- They are still walking around your environment looking for another opportunity to repossess you.
- Their assignment is to destroy you like they did to others in your family, class or area. So, you have to be careful in all that you do.

- As a believer, you have to be abstemious, not addicted to anything or allow anything have rule over you which is against God's word.
- Do things moderately without going to the extreme. With this, you will not give the devil a place in your life to re-enter you again.
- That's what it means to keep vigilant watch over your life.
- Guide your heart against any occult practice and destroy any satanic property in your possession.
- Avoid close relationship, friendship with sinful neighbors, friends and relations; yet live peaceably with them as much as possible.
- If you follow this advice, God's Spirit will remain in you and you can cast out demons anywhere.
- Your body will be the property of God and He will defend you at all times.
- With a life of righteousness, any time problem comes, they will see a danger sign all over you.
- They will see the name of Christ in you and the wise demons will run away (Matthew 12:43-45).
- Guide your heart against any occult practice and destroy any satanic property in your possession.
- Avoid close relationship, friendship with sinful neighbors, friends and relations; yet live peaceably with them as much as possible (Romans 8:11; Mark 16:17-18).
- If any foolish demon tries to attack you, you will cast them out.
- If they resist, you will burst in tongues and they will bow and surrender to the authority of Christ in you.

You need to get a copy of my book titled, "21/40 nights of decrees and your enemies will surrender".

KEEPING YOUR DELIVERANCE

- If you maintain your deliverance, you are entitled to tread upon serpents and scorpions and over all the powers of the enemy and nothing shall by any means hurt you.
- With this title deed, and authority, no problem will last long in your life.
- All believers are authorized to destroy demons and the diseases they carry (Luke 10:19; 9:1).
- The powers behind the problems in the world put together is less than the power Christ gave to a single believer.
- Finally, believers are entitled to use the name of Christ to ask anything (John 14:12-14; Matthew 18:18, 19).
- If you ask with faith, not doubting, you will receive because your well-being glorifies Christ's name on earth.
- If you ask rightly with the name of Christ, God will happily release the answer.
- Believers can bind and loose anything and no other power can stop it.
- The heavenly host is waiting for sinless believers to bind or loose and they will place a heavenly seal upon it.
- No power from any satanic kingdom can see a heavenly seal and tamper with it.

- The devil cannot authorize any demon, evil spirit or his agents to approach a heavenly seal, how much more touch it.
- I advise you, while others are seeking for money, silver; gold and other things, seek for this power.
- With this power, Peter conquered a problem that lasted for forty years.
- With this power you can walk into a class of people you never dreamt of in life.
- With this power, you can gather wealth and riches.
- With this power, you can speak to proud demons and say, hold your peace and come out and they will obey.
- With this power, you can do practically anything and nothing can stop you.
- With this power, all your problems will bow and surrender forever.

I AM THAT I AM

- In answer to Moses' question, God answered and said, "I AM THAT I AM" is my name.
- He told Moses that He appeared to Abraham, Isaac and Jacob by the name of God Almighty, but not by his name JEHOVAH.
- None of the fathers of faith- Abraham, Isaac or Jacob knew God by the name JEHOVAH.
- The meaning of JEHOVAH as translated in the Old Testament is the covenant God (Acts 3:6-8; Exodus 3:14; 6:3; Revelation 1:4).
- JEHOVAH means the one who was and is to come, the eternal one.
- God can never change. He is immutable and no situation or circumstance can change Him.
- Right from the beginning, He laid the foundation of the earth, and heaven is his handiwork.
- God cannot get old, weak or be destroyed; He is JEHOVAH and remains God (Hebrews 1:10-12).
- Other things will wax old as garment and perish, but God remains the way He is. God existed before any mountain (Psalms 90:2; 102:24-27).
- God is older than the oldest because He created all things.
- You need to know this God because lack of the knowledge of Him will hinder your deliverance and deny you of great things.
- Great people who don't know God can be taken away in the midst of their joy or progress.

- But believers will be taken away from joy to eternal joy and everlasting peace.
- We are surrounded by powers that hate our existence and our only savior is this God.
- In all generation, He remains God and can never change because His nature is unchangeable.
- What He said yesterday is unchangeable because even His word is God that changeth not.
- By telling Moses that He is the "I AM THAT I AM" means that his promises to Moses will be fulfilled, no matter how strong Pharaoh is.
- By introducing Himself to Moses with his name "I AM THAT I AM" means, I will not stop or end until I finish Pharaoh.

GOD'S CALL TO STOP BELIEVERS' CRIES

- God was serious when He told Moses to confront Pharaoh and tell him, 'Let my people go'.
- He wants to stop the cries of the children of Israel and take them to the Promised Land.
- Now, God is no longer talking to the children of Israel but you.
- He wants to stop your oppression and deliver you from whatever bondage you are in now.
- He wants to visit the garden of your life and kill every serpent in it.
- He wants you to start building the ark of your salvation because you must not die in the evil flood.

- God wants to take you away before Sodom is destroyed (Malachi 3:6; 3:17; Exodus 3:7-8).
- God wants to promote you above all that hate and wish you dead.
- He will cause your enemies to come and bow down before you.
- All your dreams of greatness must come to pass and you will rule over all your enemies.

THE PURPOSE OF THIS PROGRAMME

- The purpose of this program is to make you great and to lift the name of God above every other name in your life.
- Whatever is called problem, oppression, etc. will bow down at the mention of His name.
- The great "I am that I am" will confront and destroy all your problems.
- In this program, all your enemies must be stopped.
- Your Pharaoh will unconditionally release you and let you go to your place in life.
- You will rise cross your red sea and walk out of all bondage.
- God will not allow you to die in this condition, no, it's not in his nature to do so.
- No more delay, no more negotiation with Pharaoh because this is your time of deliverance.
- This is time to awake, to put on your strength and your beautiful garment.
- You must shake off anything that is holding you down and walk out in freedom (Genesis 50:18-21; Exodus 12:30-33).

- You must arise for the light of your deliverance has come and the name of God "I AM THAT I AM" is standing before your Pharaoh.

Let's talk about God's names for your deliverance in our next topic.

GOD'S REDEMPTIVE NAMES FOR YOUR DELIVERANCE

- In God's plan to deliver man from the bondage of the devil, He revealed Himself through some names (Isaiah 60:1).
- The first one in my list is JEHOVAH JIREH, which means "The Lord will Provide"
- Immediately the devil saw that Abraham was going to oppose his kingdom, he attacked his wife Sarah with barrenness.
- The devil hates and fights anyone that has a covenant with God, so he attacked Abraham.
- Not only did he attack him with barrenness, but he also attacked him with lack and influenced him to go to Egypt for help (Genesis 22:13-14).
- Your own famine may be different from Abraham's, but the truth is that famine here represent problems.
- Without asking God for a way out, he went down to Egypt.
- On his arrival, he told a lie and compelled his wife to follow suit being that he was operating out of divine coverage.
- Though he later escaped famine, yet the barrenness refused to go until his old age.
- But Abraham was consistently walking with God until God intervened and blessed him with a son called Isaac at his old age.
- Much later, God asked Abraham to give him back the child through burnt sacrifice.
- As he presented his only son Isaac for a sacrifice in obedience, God Himself provided a ram in place of Isaac instead.

- That's the first time the name JEHOVAH JIREH came, meaning the Lord our provider (Genesis 12:10-13, 18; 21:1-3).
- If you repent and cue into God's covenant, God will provide all your needs and provide you a way of escape from all your problems.
- So, as you pray having in mind the name "JEHOVAH JIREH" all your problems will be solved.
- "JEHOVAH JIREH" will provide and make a way where there's no way as you get involved in this program (Genesis 22:7-8, 13-14).
- When you give your life to God through Christ, He can give you anything, no matter the size.
- Deliverance gets easy when you abandon your life to Christ and pray in faith.
- For God to send His only son to come and die for us is serious evidence that every other thing can and will be provided for us through Christ (John 4:10; 3:16).
- So, once you link up with Christ through repentance, everything will be provided.
- Another name that is very important is "JEHOVAH SHALOM" meaning, "The Lord our Peace" (Judges 6.24).
- During the days of Gideon, the Midianites tormented them for seven years (Judges 6:23-24).
- It was so bad that everyone in Israel was practically living in fear both inside their own houses and in their farm land.
- When Gideon eventually encountered God, he became so much terrified, but God assured him of peace and life.

- From that day, God's presence brought peace and abundant life to believers on earth and much more at the appearance of Christ.
- So, when you are in trouble or suffering from fear and all manner of demonic harassment unto death, call upon JEHOVAH SHALOM and peace will show up.
- God allowed His only begotten son Jesus Christ to be wounded or chastised so that we can have peace.
- Don't forget, it is by His stripes that we ARE healed, NOT 'will be' healed (Isaiah 53:5; Colossians 1:20).
- If you understand the full reason why Christ accepted the stripes, you will not allow sickness and disease to feast on any part of your body.
- The shedding of the blood of Jesus Christ on the cross brought peace into every believer's life.
- I hope you understand the kind of peace I am talking about?
- The next redemptive name for our deliverance is "JEHOVAH TSIDKENU", meaning, "The Lord our righteousness".
- This name is found in Jeremiah 23:6, where it refers to the future Messiah who will reign in righteousness.
- A day is coming in this present world when righteousness will reign without resistance under the government of Christ for one thousand years (Jeremiah 23:6).
- At that time, the children of Israel and all believers washed by the blood of Christ will live safely.
- To be a partaker of this kingdom, you must get born again now and begin to practice righteousness.

- So, I counsel you to receive Christ, remain in Him and pray fervently to enjoy the righteousness of Christ here and now.
- The next redemptive name for our deliverance is "JEHOVAH RAPHA" or "JEHOVAH ROPHEKA" which means, "The Lord healeth us" or "I am the Lord thy Physician" (1 Corinthians 1:30).
- This name is found in Exodus 15:26, where God declares Himself as the healer of Israel if they obey His commandments.
- After the deliverance of the children of Israel from the bondage of Egypt, they were so happy (Exodus 15:26; Isaiah 53:4-5).
- When they saw the great work of God, Miriam who was the sister of Moses led them in praise and worship; and all Israel praised God (Exodus 15:1-22).
- But when they came to a place called Marah where they encountered bitter water, they forgot all the goodness of God and murmured against Moses.
- At that point, Moses prayed and God showed him a tree and immediately he cast it into the water, the water became sweet; that tree is Christ.
- No matter your present situation, even if you are at the point of death, never you murmur against God or his servant.
- You need to believe God for your deliverance and pray in faith. It was in Marah that God entered into the covenant of healing with the children of Israel.
- Today, God is calling you into a covenant of healing and if you respond now, you will receive both divine healing and divine health.
- All you need is to repent, acknowledge your sins, stop complaining or shifting blames.

- Listen to God's voice, not the voice of your problems or anything that contradicts His word.
- Do the right thing, obey God's commandment; keep his words as much as you can and your deliverance will be made accessible (Exodus 15:23-26).
- He promised to exempt you from diseases and every problem that wastes others.
- What Christ did on the cross is enough to put every obedient believer out of grief and sorrow.
- The devil has no legal right to afflict, torment or oppress believers who know their right.
- Jesus was stricken, smitten and afflicted so that we can be freed from every problem.
- He was wounded, bruised, chastised and beaten with stripes for believers to have peace, be healed and remain in health.
- The word you are hearing now is enough to stir up faith in you, bring healing to your body and keep you healthy for the rest of your life.
- God allowed Jesus to receive stripes in order to destroy our infirmities and our sickness.
- Another name for our deliverance is, JEHOVAH NISSI, which simple means; "The Lord our banner", "The Lord our victory" or "The Lord our captain" (Matthew 8:16-17; 1 Peter 2:24).
- This name is found in Exodus 17:15, where Moses builds an altar and declares it as a memorial to Jehovah Nissi after the Israelites' victory over the Amalekites.

- This redemptive name came when the Amalek fought against the children of Israel in the wilderness, after they left Egypt.
- It was their first battle after they left Egyptian bondage.
- At that time, Moses choose Joshua and other soldiers to defend the children of Israel (Exodus 17:15).
- At the end of the battle, God gave the children of Israel victory.
- Right there, Moses built an altar and called it, "JEHOVAH NISSI, meaning; "The Lord is our banner, victory and captain".
- What a privilege to have God as your banner, victory and captain in this violent world we live in.
- No wonder why Israel won almost every battle of their life thereafter.
- In the reference above, they defeated the Canaanites and utterly destroyed their cities.
- When they came to the Amorites, they smote them with the edge of the sword and possessed their land from Aron unto Jabbok (Numbers 21:21-32; Deuteronomy 2:24-25 Joshua 10:12-14).
- When they fought Bashan, they smote them until there was no survival and they possessed their land (Numbers 21:33-35; Deuteronomy 3:1-18).
- The Midianites came out with determination to fight them but the children of Israel slew all the males under the banner of the Lord (Numbers 25:16-18; 31:1-24, 48-54).
- When God is your banner, victor or captain, you will never be defeated as long as you remain loyal to Him.

- When they came to Jericho, there was a strong roadblock against the children of Israel.
- That's to tell you that no matter how close you are to God, one day, the enemy will block your way (Numbers 21:1-3).
- Even now, it may be possible that your way is blocked and you are really suffering.
- When their way to the Promised Land was blocked, they prayed to God for direction.
- As soon as they received divine instruction, the impossibility became possible.
- You cannot continue to lose battles when the Lord becomes your banner, victor or captain (Numbers 21:1-3).
- You need to invoke the power attached to JEHOVAH NISSI and all your problems will bow before our captain.
- The next redemptive name in line is "JEHOVAH SHAMMAH" which means, "The Lord is Present" or "The Lord is there".
- This name is found in Ezekiel 48:35, where it describes the future city of Jerusalem as "The Lord is There.
- "In that chapter, we are presented with the life in the eternal city where God will be manifesting without interruption.
- Even now as a believer, God will manifest in your situation as you cue into this program.
- God also promised all believers who keep his commandment of his ever-abiding presence even till the end of the world.

- God's name "ADONAI" which is translated "MASTER or LORD" implies ruler-ship over his creation (Ezekiel 48:35; Matthew 28:20; 18:19).
- God has absolute dominion and in Him is the ability to guide aright the affairs of men who are obedient to his commandments.
- Let's move on and discuss our father's attributes.

OUR FATHER'S ATTRIBUTES

- There are some inherent characteristic and qualities that pertain to God alone, which He doesn't share with any mortal.
- When He enters into such office, no one dares to enter or share such place with Him (Exodus 23:17).
- We are talking about, God the father, the son and the Holy Ghost.
- First, let us discuss the fatherhood of God to all believers who are qualified to be sons by reason of receiving Jesus Christ as their Lord and savior.
- God is the father of all believers through the covenant of redemption.
- You are therefore required to commune with Him bearing in mind that you are talking to your father who created all things and also able to do all things (Matthew 6:6, 8, 32).
- Before you ask God anything you must be convinced that He is your father and that He would love to do anything to make you happy as his child.

- If God sees you as his child, you must recognize Him also as your father.
- You should approach God as a child in prayer, not like a slave before his master.
- The reason why many ask and don't receive is because they are not really God's children by redemption.
- Even some of the redeemed are not bold, so when they ask, they don't receive because they ask in doubt (Matthew 7:7-11).
- If you are born again and truly know your right, you will get whatever you ask when approach God in faith ready to receive.
- No true believer will seek God genuinely and fail to find Him; and if you knock, it shall be opened to you (Matthew 7:7).
- This is what we call waiting upon the Lord, which is the subject of consideration.
- But before you can wait effectively, you must know Him and believe that He is your father.
- You must know his names, attributes and be convinced that He is your father.
- Other things you have to know is that your heavenly father is better, richer and more willing to answer your prayers than your earthly father.
- He is more ready to help you more than all the good fathers on earth can help their loving children.
- You cannot ask your earthly father for bread and he will give you a stone, never.

- No good earthly father can give his loving child a serpent instead of a fish.
- If it's rare and almost impossible for a sinful earthly father to refuse to give their children what they ask, then our heavenly father will never refuse to answer you when you pray.
- Moreover, your earthly father may not even have what their earthly children ask for.
- But our heavenly father has all that we will ever ask and is ever willing to give us more than we can ever ask.
- To fear God means, to have respect for his words and commandment.
- It's to do everything possible even in the face of death to obey Him and stand against anything that opposes his word (Matthew 7:8; Psalms 103:13).
- If you have respect for your father, you will do everything possible to keep his rules; that's what we mean by fearing God.
- Believers who keep God's commandment are bold to ask for anything, and it will be given to them.
- There's a level to which you get to in your relationship with your heavenly father and you will begin to receive certain things even before you ask (Luke 15:20-24, 31).
- There's a level of consecration you have with a determination to remain faithful to God, and you will get more than you ask.
- Understand that all that God has belongs to you. It's an insult for a child of God to live like a slave, to accept poverty or failure.
- All that God has, everything good belongs to believers even before they ask.

THREE

QUALIFICATION OF GOD'S CHILDREN AND WRONG PRAYERS

- ☐ True children resemble their parents not only physically but in character also.
- ☐ So, to prove that you are a child of God, you must behave like God in character and have his nature.
- ☐ In times of prayer, God's children can pray all manner of prayer, both judgmental and mercy. But if the rebellious repent, they will obtain mercy.
- ☐ Putting on the whole armor of God means, being equipped with all the weapons of warfare to stop any determined enemy that has vowed to terminate your life or divine program before time (Ephesians 6:10-18).
- ☐ It means, being able to stop Saul-like satanic agents before they get to our Damascus to kill us (Acts 9:1-11).

ALL MANNER OF PRAYERS

- Believers must not allow Saul-like satanic agents to threaten and fulfill their threats on them.
- We must gather together to pray against evil threats even if it means getting them blinded to provoke their conversion.
- Praying all manner of prayers presents two options to satanic determined agents.
- For Saul, his own was blindness or conversion that led to his call to ministry, life or death.
- Believers must be strong in the Lord; put on the whole armor of God to match up with the wiles of the devil and his agents.
- If you don't pray all manner of prayer, satanic agents may not receive the arrow of blindness and the option of repentance, deliverance or divine call.
- If you don't pray all manner of prayer, Saul will fulfill his threats against the Damascus believers and the apostles will not receive power to continue their ministry (Acts 9:8; 4:29).
- If you pray only prayer of mercy, satanic agents will carry on with their mission unchallenged.
- Many of them like Saul will never be blinded unto repentance for divine call.
- If you pray only judgmental prayer, Saul-like agents will all be blinded unto death without experiencing divine mercy.
- That's why we need to allow the Holy Spirit to intercede for us when we don't know what to pray as we should.
- In times of confusion and weakness, when you don't know what to pray, you must allow the Holy Spirit to help you.

- Only the Spirit of God can rightly pray in times of confusion and believers' weakness.
- He knows every repentant Paul and the unrepentant Ananias and Sapphira because only Him can search the hearts.
- Only the Holy Spirit knows what's in the mind of the Spirit and only Him can rightly pray according to the will of God.
- No matter your length of experience in the Lord, you can never be perfect and knowledgeable as God's Spirit (Acts 9:6, 8; 1-2; 4:29-31; Romans 8:26-27).
- Even if you think you are vast in knowledge, having travelled far and near, very spiritual and eloquent, won many battles; remember, you are not the Holy Spirit.
- With your unenlightened mind and human limitations, you can make mistakes but God's Spirit cannot.
- Samuel with all his prophetic gifts almost anointed Eliab instead of David. Look at what the word of God said in; (Acts 10:9-20; 16:6-10; Isaiah 58:8; 2 Corinthians 3:5; Job 8:9 and Proverbs 3:5-7).
- Now, what is God's decision for believers who sincerely pray amiss-wrongly and ignorantly?
- We need to know this because man in his best state equals to vanity when compared with the Almighty (Jeremiah 10:23; 1 Samuel 16:6, 7; Isaiah 42:16, 19, 20).
- There was a time that Jeremiah was praying earnestly for God's mercy for the unrepentant children of Israel.
- It was a wrong prayer and God asked him to stop.
- Praying all manner of prayer or knowing what you are supposed to pray but deciding to pray wrongly is not acceptable to God.

- It's wrong to pray for your enemies to die when you are supposed to pray for their repentance.
- However, God may not reject you if you pray wrongly when you are ignorant.
- If you pray aright, God will hear you and answer you but if you pray wrongly, He will not answer you.
- It's better to pray aright and when you don't know what to pray, speak in tongues (Romans 8:26-27; Psalms 39:5-6; Jeremiah 7:15-16).
- We are moving forward to the next series with a topic titled, praying with love, not with hatred.

PRAYING WITH LOVE, NOT WITH HATE

- Whether you are praying in weakness or in confusion, you must have God's kind of love in your heart.
- God's kind of love will not want any sinner to perish or die in their wickedness.
- However, God doesn't force anyone because of their right of choice making.
- Everyone has the freedom of choice to serve God or the devil, to repent or to die in sin (Joshua 24:15; Jeremiah 18:7-10; Matthew 23:37-38; Revelation 22:17).
- The truth is that whether you pray for your enemies to die or live, repent or perish, succeed or fail, one thing must happen because of the right of choice.
- But the most important thing is that believers must have God's kind of love in their heart.
- In the New Testament dispensation, hatred is totally out of place in the life of believers (Deuteronomy 30:19-20; Matthew 5:43-48).
- We must not pray with hatred in the heart, no matter the kind of prayer you engage in.
- Believers are commanded to love their enemies, bless them that curse us and do good to them that hate us.
- We are also commanded to pray for those who despitefully use us and persecute us.

- How do we interpret the above command? For me, it is to put away hatred from our hearts, pray all kinds of prayer and do the right thing at all times to all people.
- Always let your motives be right; do all things, including prayers without hypocrisy.
- Pray without regarding iniquity in your heart; forgive all that offended you and pray according to God's will in faith.
- Genuine love of God in the heart allows God's Spirit to dwell in us freely.
- This doesn't mean that believers should assist a drunkard to get drunk or drug addicts to get worse.
- Your child can offend you but don't hate him or her to the extent of wishing him or her death.
- So, when I say "die" in my prayers, what I mean is breaking away of the power behind the evil action.
- Witches, sinners and law breakers who refuse to allow the spirit behind their evil action to break will die or separate with the demonic spirit.
- I strongly believe that no amount of fall and die prayers can kill any determined witch, wizard, sinner or law breaker who is determined to repent (Luke 11:11-13).
- Ananias argued with God and would have preferred that Paul should remain blind or even die but God rejected his desire.
- Ananias was a true child of God but his knowledge was limited about Paul.
- He only knew about Paul's satanic assignment but nothing about God's call upon his life.

- ☐ He was a disciple in Damascus with the details of Paul's mission to cart away believers for execution.
- ☐ He must have led the Damascus believers to pray that God should strike Paul with blindness and possibly kill him.
- ☐ They all saw Paul as an unrepentant wizard who must die by God's fire.
- ☐ They must have prayed and declared death for anyone who would not allow evangelism to move forward in Damascus.
- ☐ The comment of one of their leaders when he heard that Paul was blind confirmed all the wishes and the desires of Damascus brethren (Acts 9:11, 13-16).
- ☐ None of them knew that he had had an encounter with Christ and was already called and had answered the divine call of God.
- ☐ They never knew that from birth, the wizard Paul was chosen by God.
- ☐ He was a chosen vessel to bear Christ's name before the Gentiles, Kings and the children of Israel.
- ☐ Though the Damascus brethren prayed against the evil agenda of Paul, yet God didn't find them guilty for their ignorance in prayers.
- ☐ He knew that they prayed according to their level of knowledge.
- ☐ He truly answered their prayers and blinded his eyes, but didn't stop his agenda for Paul after he repented. He was determined to show him great things he must suffer for His names sake and Paul obliged.

THE PRAYERS OF A REPENTANT WIZARD

- ☐ When King Ahab heard God's word after murdering Naboth, the Jezreelite, he repented in sack clothes and in ashes.
- ☐ He started fasting until God changed his judgment against him.
- ☐ It is right to teach people how to pray aright. But you must be careful not to backslide while trying to correct believers who ignorantly pray like the Damascus brethren or Prophet Jeremiah.
- ☐ Pray as you are led, with a perfect heart, full of divine love without hatred or an unforgiving spirit (Matthew 18:21-35; Mark 11:25-26; Luke 6:35-37; Acts 9:10-14; 1 Kings 21:25-29; Jeremiah 7:15-16

Turn with me to the next series - God's attributes.

FOUR

GOD'S ATTRIBUTES 1

Don't forget that we were talking about fasting or waiting upon the LORD before we backed off a little to talk about who He is, His names and His nature.

Now let's talk about his attributes. According to;

- God is "INFINITE". He is everywhere at all times and in every situation.
- He is eternal with no beginning and no ending. No one can run away from God or go to where he cannot be located by God because He is everywhere.
- Before you were born, He was and is and will forever be (Psalms 139:7-12).
- In heaven, ever before He created heaven, God was and after the creation, He still is and will ever be as He is.

- God is in hell and He is the only person that the fire in hell cannot affect.
- No matter the speed of the fastest aircraft and other creatures which possess the strength of the morning in the air, they are as slow as the snail even in their fastest motion.
- The fastest movement in the sea is slower in speed because before they think of moving, God is already there in a split of time.
- God's hand can reach to the ends of the earth and go beyond the places that science has not known or will ever know.
- All the activities of the powers in the dark kingdom are more exposed to God than the brightest of day.
- Night and day cannot hide anything from God, so it's foolishness to think that there is a secret you can hide from God.
- In the presence of God, darkness exposes everything in it (Psalms 9:2).
- It's a great privilege to know that you can communicate with God from wherever you are and He answers immediately.
- Our God is the highest, can never be brought under and has never been brought under.
- This is the God that says we should wait on Him, the most high that is higher than the highest.
- He is the Most blessed and Potentate, who only hath immortality; to whom be honor and power forever.
- The four-beast rest not day and night, saying, Holy, holy, LORD; God Almighty…

Note that the word translated "beast" in Revelation 13:1 is "thereon" and that means "vicious, wild beast" referring to the antichrist (Revelation 4:8, 11).

But "this four-living creature" are representatives of angelic beings (Ezekiel 1:5, 10, 13, 14; 10:12, 14, 15, 20 and Isaiah 6:1-4).

- There are different orders of angels. They all worship God and minister to the holiness of God. They praise God saying, "So finally, God gets all the glory'.
- Fallen angels and fallen men are forever banished from heaven. All rebels are out of sight.
- Holy angels and redeemed men now worship God.
- They pour unceasing praise unto God in worship and adoration (Revelation 5:9-14; 7:9-12; 11:16, 17; 19:1-9).
- Another attribute of God is that "GOD IS ALL WISE" and there's no problem He cannot solve.
- It's indisputable that the earth and all that is in it emanated from God.
- His works are manifold and He made them by his wisdom.
- He founded the earth in his wisdom without any contribution from evil forces and other creatures.
- In his understanding, He established the heavens without any human assistance.
- The wisdom of all the scientists with all their discoveries put together is lighter than nothing before a dot of God's wisdom (Revelation 4:8-11; Psalms 104:24; Proverbs 3:19).

- Wisdom and might exclusively belong to God without any argument by any force.
- God only, can change times and seasons. He has removed powerful Kings and can remove any King without notice or negotiation.
- He sets Kings, gives wisdom unto the wise and knowledge to them that lack understanding.
- Because He created all and owns all, He can give to those who ask Him.
- He can make the most foolish person wise and make the wisest among men foolish.
- None owns anything that was not given to him by the owner and the creator of all.
- He knows everything from the root because nothing exists without his knowledge.
- No one owns anything permanently; He gives and takes because the depth of the riches is only determined by Him.
- He doesn't share wisdom, knowledge and understanding with any, He owns all and gives to whoever He wants to give.
- This is the God that says that we should ask, seek, and knock.
- It's not a waste of time to wait on Him and that is why you need to know Him before waiting on Him.
- Seeking for wisdom, knowledge, understanding or anything outside of God is the greatest mistake anyone can make on earth.
- God is wisdom personified. James, a true servant of God told the twelve tribes of Israel who were scattered abroad to focus their

seeking of wisdom only in God (Daniel 2:20-21; Romans 11:33; Colossians 2:23; James 1:5).

- He said, if anyone lacks wisdom, let him ask God and that is what we must do in this program.
- God who sees the end from the beginning through his servant James gives you an express invitation to ask Him for wisdom.

THE ALL POWERFUL OMINIPOTENT, INFINITE GOD

- In our search for divine attributes, "GOD IS OMNIPOTENT" meaning that "GOD IS ALL POWERFUL"
- In the beginning, before life began, He was and all things were created by Him, including the heaven and earth.
- In the beginning God created the heaven and the earth (Genesis 1:1; Exodus 15:17).
- This earns Him the title "OMINIPOTENT GOD". People who are short-sighted, who lack knowledge or know God seek for power outside Him.
- What made Moses great and powerful is not his physical strength or his educational qualification, but his intimate relationship with God (Deuteronomy 3:24; 1 Chronicles 16:25).
- When Moses discovered who God is and the power in His name, he surrendered to Him.
- When he surrendered all that, he learnt from the Egyptian occult house for God's knowledge, he became great.
- Every greatness outside divine knowledge is useless and will fade away with time.
- It's unprofitable to waste time seeking to get anything outside God.
- Immediately Moses proved that the Personality sending him back to Pharaoh is greater than Pharaoh, his faith was built up.
- You can challenge any problem with God's name and win victoriously.

- Through his name, everything you need can be provided and no sorrow is attached to his provision.
- Through God's name, you can have peace, righteousness, divine presence and dominion over sin.
- God is a father to all that find Him through Christ and He empowers them with his own righteousness.
- When you cue into His will and plan through Christ, He will never leave you nor forsake you.
- That's why He is called the "INFINITE GOD", eternal, with no beginning and no ending.
- He is the all-wise God, and none has this attribute. He only can solve all problems because He sees the end from the beginning and nothing is hidden from Him.
- His decision is always right, He had never made any mistake and none can find Him guilty. God's Attributes 2 is our next topic.

FIVE

GOD'S ATTRIBUTES 2

THE ADMINISTRATIVE GIFT OF MOSES' AND DAVID'S WISDOM

- He is all-wise and can make you wiser than you are now.
- When He showed Moses his greatness, Moses automatically became great.
- He touched Moses with his mighty hand and everything that Moses ever touched became prosperous.
- This is the God that we are about to wait on, please you are invited to join us.
- If you accept Him as your captain or banner, you can never lose any battle in life.
- No decision on earth is complete without the decision to follow Him, serve Him and allow Him to lead you.

- When David, the son of Jesse accepted Him and submitted to His leadership, he defeated every enemy including the Goliath of his generation.
- Because he submitted to divine wisdom, God made him brave, courageous in battle before any enemy.
- Not only that, God made him skillful and very intimidating before his enemies.
- With these qualities from the all-wise God, David led the children of Israel to subdue the Philistines, Canaanites, Moabites, Ammonites, Arameans, Edomites and the Amalekites.
- Because he submitted himself to divine wisdom, he became a renowned army general, a champion of war who never lost any battle.
- David's submission to divine authority helped him to conquer the supposedly impregnable Jebusite city of Jerusalem and made it his capital (Job 40:2; 42:2).
- If you submit to God's wisdom, no enemy will prevail over you; try it.
- Do you know that it was King David who started the business of slaying giants in Israel before other army officers followed suit?
- All the powers standing as giants in your place of birth or workplace can be slain if you submit to divine wisdom and authority (2 Samuel 5:4-7; 2 Samuel 21:15-21).
- You will raise soldiers like David who can do what you can longer do, go to where you cannot go even at your old age.

- One of the secrets of King David was that he regarded and fought Israel's enemies as God's enemies and dedicated his spoils of war unto the Lord.
- But the major secret was his submission to God's will, His wisdom and authority.
- His submission to divine wisdom made him the greatest King in Israel with an unusual wisdom in administration (2 Samuel 2:5-7; 3:32-37; 2 Samuel 5:1-4).
- David in his administrative wisdom, he mastered the right manner of approach on how to carry everyone along.
- He spoke to his subjects with wisdom and as a result, they became extremely loyal and devoted to him.
- By his divine wisdom, even his enemies find it difficult and almost impossible to identify his faults.
- He was the accepted shepherd boy, the harp player who played harp to calm the troubled spirit of King Saul.
- In his submission to divine wisdom, he became the warrior who slew Goliath in his youth and became the hero of his people.
- Later, he became the King, who reigned first at Hebron and thereafter, at Jerusalem over all Israel.
- By divine wisdom, his reign was totally free from idolatry because he was loyal to God.
- By divine wisdom, he built a palace, opened highways, trade routes and secured the prosperity of the kingdom materially.
- David was a man of deep piety, contrition and close communion with God.

- He esteemed the presence of God above every earthly treasure and sought for God's leading before any major decision.
- David never joked with his relationship with God or trade his position in heaven with any material thing. He valued God's presence above every other (Psalms 84:10, 11; 1 Samuel 23:10-11; 2 Samuel 2:1; Isaiah 40:12-15).
- He never depended on his human wisdom but always enquired from the Lord for guidance before action.
- To maintain his relationship with God, he forgives his offenders.
- David understood very well like Job did that no thought can be withheld from God's wisdom.

SEARCH FOR THE ALPOWERFUL GOD

- As we continue to search for divine attribute, we discover that God is "ALL POWERFUL, OMINIPOTENT".
- He gathered the whole waters on earth in the hollow of his hand.
- He meted out heaven with the span and comprehended the dust of the earth in a measure.
- He weighed the mountains in a scale and the hills in a balance.
- This is the God that the devil and his deceived agents fight against.
- In his power, He teaches the wise wisdom, but none can teach Him.
- He counsels all, instructs all and none can counsel or instruct Him because man in his best is all together lighter than nothing in wisdom before the LORD.
- In the path of knowledge, understanding and justice, the best among the professors depends on Him to learn.
- What man describes as big is small in the eyes of God because the nations put together are as a drop in a bucket.
- They are counted as the smallest dust when measured in divine balance.
- When He takes up the isles, they are very little in size as nothing in description.
- No man can fathom the powerfulness of God because they will fail in their comprehension.
- This is the God that people doubt his ability when they pray because they lack knowledge of whom He is.

- This is the God who says, "wait for me, seek me and you will find me".
- This is the God I want to introduce to you and those who seek Him will find Him (Jeremiah 32:17; Daniel 4:35; Matthew 19:26).
- Look at the heaven and earth; they were made by God without any contribution from any power outside God.
- There's absolutely nothing that God cannot do and with Him on your side, all things are possible.
- The reputation of the bests among men are reputed as nothing before Him.
- The wisest among men is as good as nothing because He can discover errors, unknown to them.
- In the army of heaven, He does anything He wants, how much more among the inhabitants of the earth.
- It's foolishness to question God's decision because His verdict is final.
- Limitations and impossibilities are the language of mortal man; these don't exist before God.
- Doubts, failures, discouragement and hopelessness is a foreign language before the 'ALL POWERFUL GOD"; they are non-existent before the Almighty.
- In times of prayer, waiting upon Him, seeking His face, make no room for fear, doubts, unbelief or discouragement.
- These are negative emotions before God; they belong to unbelievers, agents of the devil and their master the devil.

- Deliverance preachers, teachers and ministers have emphasized so much about the powers of the devil, which may be true; but the "POWER OF GOD" dominants every other power.
- It is important to note that the power the devil has belongs to God. But it is corrupt, defiled and contaminated the day he rebelled against the Almighty (Jude 6, 8; Revelation 15:3).
- Believers who are schooled in the school of "GOD'S POWER have nothing to do with negative circumstances, fear, doubts, unbelief and discouragement.
- Because of their new orientation about who God is, His names and attributes, they don't have respect for impossibilities.
- Also, they know that if prayers are not answered, it can never be from God's side.
- They look for the fault from outside God because God has no relationship with failure.
- He is more willing to answer our prayers, to give, to bless and to perform miracles, signs and wonders more than we are willing to ask or receive.
- Believers in school of "PRAYER AND POWER" sing the song of Moses the servant of God and the song of the Lamb.
- Moses never joined the defeated all his life or waste time with the faithless. He fought and conquered and our Lord Jesus did much more than Moses.

THE OMNIPRESENT GOD

- Another divine attribute which no creature can share with God is His "OMNIPRESENT" nature.
- This means that "GOD IS PRESENT EVERYWHERE" at all times.
- This particular attribute of God confirms that nothing can be hidden from God.
- All things are naked before Him because with God, there's no secret under the heavens.
- It's the believers' joy to know that the God we serve is everywhere with us to defend us (Genesis 28:15, 16; Joshua 2:11; Psalms 139:7-12).
- When it's like we are left alone in the midst of enemies or problems, our comfort should be that we are not alone.
- When we are sleeping, even in the midst of enemies, He is with us and can never leave us alone.
- Jacobs's testimony as a fugitive, a runaway boy in the middle of the bush was, "Surely the LORD is in this place and I knew it not".
- There's no place you can get to and God will be absent or late in arrival.
- He is always everywhere before we get there and can never be taken unawares.
- You may keep secrets from mortal men but nothing is a secret before God; He's aware of it and can never be taken by surprise.
- That's why you must not be afraid of anything as long as you do the right thing.

- The heathen, all your enemies may rage and imagine evil against you but once God is on your side, their plan is as good as nothing.
- They may take counsel against you, but God will laugh at them because before execution; the Lord will have them in derision.
- Believers who contend for their faith are comfortable in the hand of God and no evil shall befall them.
- We are not done, let's proceed, God's Attributes still continues.

SIX

GOD'S ATTRIBUTES 3

- Another attribute of God is "PERFECT IN KNOWLEDGE", meaning that He knows everything before they became known.
- He telleth the number of the stars; he calleth them all by their names - Psalm 147:4).
- The best professors of mathematics, accountants and all that are trained in understanding numbers cannot count the stars in the heavens.
- But in split seconds, God can count them and call them by names because He created them and they report to Him daily.
- You may be deficient in hearing but the creator doesn't experience failure in hearing. In his perfect knowledge, He hears the faintest words.
- He knows your thoughts before you start thinking about it and can discern your imaginations.
- All the ears of all creatures put together are not functional compared to God's hearing ability.

- His eyes can see beyond the darkest realm because the darkness is like light before Him (Psalms 147:4; 94:9-11).
- He created knowledge that he gave to men, so no knowledge could be hidden from Him.
- All knowledge, negative or positive reports to God who owns it ever before they resume operation.
- The acclaimed owners of knowledge are not the rightful owners and cannot serve them without getting approval from the creator.
- To retain God's knowledge and benefit from it without failure, you must acknowledge the creator and serve Him through the Lord Jesus (Luke 16:15).
- You may hide your true character from people but not from God.
- God knows your down-sitting, your uprising and your thoughts ever before they come to you.
- Any path you take in life- where you go to or where you will ever be are known by God.
- Everything that is called human knowledge, gathered together can be pocketed by God without stress.
- The so-called wise people who have no reference to God through Christ are regarded as foolish before God.
- If you wish to discover any secret, you can ask, seek, and knock through waiting on God. God knows where all earthly secrets are hiding now.
- All impossibilities are without any clue because their secrets have not been exposed by God (Luke 16:15).

- Ebola and all incurable diseases still thrive because their secrets are yet to be discovered.
- The devil and his agents have secrets that empower them to do evil, but only God knows those secrets. Yes. It does.
- If you join us to wait on God in prayer, you can discover the secrets behind your problems (Luke 16:15).

ENCOUNTER WITH CHRIST

- Once the secret behind any problem is discovered, their strength collapses and dies.
- The woman of Samaria knew nothing about science but she knew something very important (John 4:22-26).
- She said that she was convinced that once the Messiah comes, He will reveal all things to her.
- That conviction kept her alive and strong until the day she met Christ and she was not disappointed.
- The day she met Christ, she left her water pot, entered into the city and announced the coming of Christ.
- In her own words she said, "Come, see a man which told me all things that I ever did: is not this the Christ?" (John 4:29).
- Those that will meet Christ in this program will discover how to solve their problems.
- Christ will tell them all that they need to know, which will set them free and give them complete deliverance.

THE IMMUTABILITY OF GOD

- The next in my list on God's attributes is "IMMUTABILITY", meaning God's nature is unchangeable (Exodus 3:14; Hebrews 1:12; Psalms 90:2; 102:24-27).
- When God told Moses that my name is "I AM THAT I AM ", He emphasized on the immutability of his name as being unchangeable.
- Like God, there's nothing like age, and He remains the same, day after day and year after year.
- Heaven and earth will one day wax old as a garment and pass away, but God remains the same.
- All the older adults and things you see around you were once very young and tender.
- The young, vibrant youth you are seeing now will one day become old and die one day because they are all given to change, but God's nature doesn't change.
- From everlasting to everlasting, God can never change. He is the same unchangeable God throughout all generations.
- The foundation of the earth all other creatures with no exception, will get old, but God will not.
- The power that will get them old is of the Lord and in His control (Malachi 3:6; John 1:17).
- Whatever that had a beginning will eventually come to an end, but our God is endless; He can end all and remain unending.

- If you want to last long, fulfill your destiny on earth, and live eternally with the unending God; it's possible.
- What you need to do is to identify yourself with God through his son Jesus Christ.
- In the Old Testament, the sons of Jacob identified with God and up till now they are not consumed.
- There's a life called eternal life preserved by God through Christ for all who will repent and remain loyal to Him till death.
- This is called in the New Testament, grace and truth which came by Jesus Christ and can only be obtained through Him.

THE FAITHFULNESS OF GOFD

- Another attribute of God is "FAITHFULNESS" which means that God is completely trustworthy.
- His word cannot fail because it's perfect (Malachi 3:6; John 1:17).
- When you cue into God's word in faith, you will not be disappointed.
- God is so faithful to watch over his word until it is fulfilled.
- It can convert negatives to positive to remain steadfast in the face of enemies.
- God's word can enter into the dividing asunder of the repented sinful soul and convert it to become holy.
- It can deliver from bondage, bring victims to liberty and bless the repentant who was once cursed (Malachi 3:6; John 1:17).

- Whatever God speaks comes to pass, no matter who stands against it because He stands to watch his words fulfilled.
- Abraham was nobody when God promised to give him the ancestral land of many strong nations.
- Those nations heard it and vowed to defend their father's land handed over to them from generation to generation.
- After the promise was made, the nation Israel, the physical children of Abraham entered into Egyptian bondage.
- They were enslaved people in that foreign land for many years, about four hundred years. But one day, God called Moses to demand for their deliverance from the Egyptians.
- They resisted God's word, but no one can succeed in resisting the Almighty.
- One day, their bondage was broken and they moved out of Egypt and lived in the wilderness under different tents for many years (Deuteronomy 2:17-19; Numbers 22:10-11; 1 Corinthians 1:9; 1 Thessalonians 5:24; Hebrews 6:18).
- You may be presently going through your wilderness experience, suffering without help.
- The children of Israel suffered extensively in the wilderness, but the presence of God was with them in those tents.
- As they moved from one tent to another, the enemies in the land heard it. People asked them where they were going to.
- And their response had always been, "We are going to the Promised Land", right from when they were in Egypt.
- They were homeless for many years under severe weather conditions- cold or hot.

- They were exposed to danger from wild animals and from trained soldiers in their Promised Land who were ready to attack them.
- Even when they were mocked at and tagged jokers, confused people and vagabonds, they held unto the promise God made to their fathers.
- Enemies from many nations rose against them, but they never prevailed over them.
- The journey was too long and full of troubles, but they eventually got to the Promised Land border.
- I don't know where you are now in your journey of life but you will get to your Promised Land.

DETERMINED ENEMIES AND THE FAITHFUL GOD

- The descendants of evil worshippers in the Promised Land were determined to stop the children of Israel from entering the land.
- They were energized by the gods their fathers served in the land for many generations.
- Just like the children of Israel, every born-again Christian has a physical Promised Land, an inheritance, a place of rest here on earth.
- If you abide in Christ's word and his words abide in you, you will get to your place in life.

- Though you may be going through your wilderness experience now- homeless or living in tents, you will not end where you are now.
- You may be a tenant, homeless or under the fire of persecution, you will surely get to your prepared place.
- You may be under the fire of contention, division or betrayal; you will surely get to your Promised Land.
- You may be suffering poverty, hardship or conspiracy; don't give up.
- Your own fire may be oppressions, injustice and denial of your right; continue in the LORD and don't give up.
- The day you got born again, God and the hosts of heavenly angels called you into fellowship with His son Jesus Christ.
- Don't break that fellowship, no matter what you are going through now (2 Timothy 2:13).
- If you want to benefit from God's faithfulness, join this fellowship.
- Fellowship with Jesus Christ the son of God is the only fellowship that will qualify you to benefit from God's faithfulness.
- God, who has called us into this fellowship, is Himself faithful in bringing us to eternal rest.
- Even in our unfaithfulness to God, He remains faithful, awaiting our turn around and fulfilling his promises to us.
- When He promised the seed of Abraham a land flowing with milk and honey, they broke fellowship with Him, but He remained faithful.

- They broke his commandment, went out and gathered manna on the Sabbath day (Exodus 16:27-31), He still remained faithful.
- Aaron built an idol and all the children of Israel ignored divine fellowship (Exodus 32:1-33), God remained faithful to his promises.
- In the wilderness, they complained and murmured against God (Numbers 11:1-10; 16:41-43), yet God kept to his promises (Hebrews 6:18; Joshua 21:43-45).
- They broke fellowship again with God when they murmured against Moses, Aaron and even against God himself (Numbers 20:1-13; 21:4-5), but God kept to his word.
- No matter what you have done or how far away you have left God, his faithfulness is forever.
- One day, with all the enemies of Israel in the land of promise, God saw faithfulness in the lives of the children of Israel and fulfilled his promise.
- They restored their fellowship with God, confessed their sins, forsook them, and the awaiting promises manifested.
- Their enemy's weapons became useless before the faithful God.
- Entering into fellowship with God and remaining faithful brings God's promises to fulfillment.
- Again, no sinner, no matter how rich, influential or powerful, can keep what he has while a faithful believer who knows his right stays out of God's blessings.
- No sinner is a permanent owner of whatever he or she has; it can be taken away at any time by the owner and the creator of the whole universe.

- ☐ True believers are the rightful heirs of God, and they have the right to every good thing on earth through inheritance.
- ☐ If you are a believer but you are suffering, get ready to enjoy.
- ☐ If you are facing hardship, it will end today as long as you are in fellowship with God and remain faithful to his words.
- ☐ This is the time to enter into a deeper relationship with God and remain faithful till the end. Something is about to happen in your life; get ready.

THANK YOU!

I'd like to use this time to thank you for purchasing my books and helping my ministry and work. Any copy of my book you buy helps to fund my ministry and family, as well as offering much-needed inspiration to keep writing. My family and I are very thankful, and we take your assistance very seriously.

You have already accomplished so much, but I would appreciate an honest review of some of my books through the link below. This is critical since reviews reflect how much an author's work is respected.

Please [click here] to leave a review on Amazon. If you're viewing from a printed version, please visit amazon.com/review/create-review?asin=B0CZV3WR19 to leave a review.

Please be aware that I read and value all comments and reviews. You can always post a review even though you haven't finished the book yet, and then edit your reviews later.

Thank you so much as you spare a precious moment of your time and may God bless you and meet you at the very point of your need.

You can also send me an email to hello@madueke.com if you encounter any difficulty while writing your review.

PRAYER M. MADUEKE'S BESTSELLING BOOKS

Click on any of the [Buy Now] buttons to view or purchase them on my website. If you're viewing from a printed version, please visit madueke.com and search for these books.

1. Dictionary of Demons & Complete Deliverance　　[Buy Now]

2. Monitoring Spirits　　[Buy Now]

3. Praying with The Blood of Jesus　　[Buy Now]

4. The Power of Speaking in Tongues　　[Buy Now]

5. Speaking Things into Existence by Faith　　[Buy Now]

6. Discerning and Defeating the Ahab & Jezebel Spirit　　[Buy Now]

7. Defeating the Python Spirit　　[Buy Now]

8. 35 Special Dangerous Decrees　　[Buy Now]

9. 21/40 Nights of Decrees and Your Enemies Will Surrender　　[Buy Now]

10. Command the Morning, Day and Night　　[Buy Now]

11. Evil Summon　　[Buy Now]

12. Overcoming & Destroying the Spirit of Rejection & Hatred [Buy Now]

13. Queen of Heaven: Wife of Satan [Buy Now]

14. The False Prophet [Buy Now]

15. Dominion Over Sickness & Disease [Buy Now]

16. The Battle Plan for Destroying Foundational Witchcraft [Buy Now]

17. The Queen of the Coast [Buy Now]

18. Dictionary of Unmerited Favor [Buy Now]

19. Prayers for Breakthrough in your Business [Buy Now]

20. A Jump From Evil Altar [Buy Now]

21. 100 Days Prayers to Wake Up Your Lazarus [Buy Now]

22. Breaking Evil Yokes [Buy Now]

23. When Evil Altars are Multiplied [Buy Now]

24. The Battle Plan for Destroying Foundational Occultism [Buy Now]

25. Prayers for Protection [Buy Now]

26. Prayers for Academic Success [Buy Now]

27. Your Dream Directory [Buy Now]

28. Prayers for Financial Breakthrough [Buy Now]

29. Destiny and Star Hunters [Buy Now]

30. Prayers to Pray during Courtship [Buy Now]

31. 91 Days Decrees to Takeover the Year [Buy Now]

32. Alone with God [Buy Now]

33. Prayers against Satanic Oppression [Buy Now]

34. Foundations Exposed [Buy Now]

35. Prayers for Deliverance [Buy Now]

36. Prayers to Heal Broken Relationship [Buy Now]

37. Prayers for Good Health [Buy Now]

38. Comprehensive Deliverance [Buy Now]

39. Prayers for College and University Students [Buy Now]

40. 40 Prayer Giants [Buy Now]

41. Divine Protection & Immunity While Sleeping [Buy Now]

42. Prayers for Fertility in your Marriage [Buy Now]

43. More Kingdoms to Conquer   [Buy Now]

44. Confront and Conquer your Enemy   [Buy Now]

45. Prayers to Raise Godly Children   [Buy Now]

4 Free Ebooks

In order to say a 'Thank You' for purchasing *Advanced Tactics in Spiritual Warfare*, I offer these books to you in appreciation. Click or type madueke.com/free-gift in your browser.

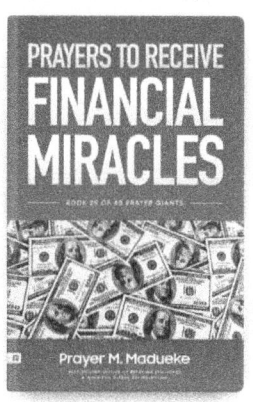

Video Bonus

I've created exclusive video content to complement the topics covered in the book. These videos provide deeper insights and discussions on the things discussed in this book, offering you a more immersive learning experience.

To access the video bonus for this course, simply click or type links.madueke.com/67ISW in your browser.

Message from the Author

I want to see you succeed, grow, and break free from negativity and obstacles. My hope is for you to thrive, unaffected by negative influences and challenging situations. Because of that, please permit me to introduce two courses that I believe passionately will help you:

1. To break the evil altars and powers of your father's house, The role of altars in the realm of existence is very key because altars are meeting places between the physical and the spiritual, between the visible and the invisible.

   Unless a man cuts off the evil flow from the power of his father's house, he will not fulfil his destiny. [Click here](#) to learn more about [my course](#) on how to tear down unholy altars and close the enemy's entryways into your life!

2. To help you seamlessly break iron-like problems, illness, delayed marriage, poverty, or any long-standing battle.

   Discover [the transformative power of Christian fasting and prayer](#). Remember, Matthew 17:21 teaches us, *"But this kind of demon does not go out except by prayer and fasting."* Ready to overcome your struggles? [Click here](#) to learn more about this course.

Embrace the journey ahead with faith, for through prayer, fasting, and the dismantling of evil altars, you shall unlock the doors to spiritual liberation and divine breakthrough. May your path be illuminated by His grace as you walk towards a life free from bondage.

If you're seeing this from the physical copy, type the link: madueke.com/courses in your browser to view all the courses on my website.

Christian Counselling

We were created for a greater purpose than only survival and God wants us to live a full life.

If you need prayer or counselling, or if you have any other inquiries, please visit the counselling page on my website to know when I will be available for a phone call.

Click or type links.madueke.com/counselling in your browser.

Let's Connect on Youtube

Join me on my YouTube channel, "Prayer M. Madueke," where I share powerful insights, guidance, and prayers for spiritual breakthroughs.

Subscribe today to unlock the secrets of the Kingdom and embrace an abundant life. Let's grow together!

Click or type links.madueke.com/youtube in your browser.

An Invitation to Become a Ministry Partner

I appreciate the support and inquiries I have received regarding collaboration with my ministry. Your prayers and dedication to the work of the Kingdom are highly valued.

You can also visit the donation page on my website if you would like to contribute or learn more about supporting my ministry: madueke.com/donate.

Thank you for your continued support and faithfulness in Christ Jesus.

www.ingramcontent.com/pod-product-compliance
Lightning Source LLC
Chambersburg PA
CBHW050914160426
43194CB00011B/2408